ROD MARTIN'S
POETIC MADNESS

POETRY FOR A NEW WORLD AND ALL EARTH'S CHILDREN

This book is for all the people I love and love to write poems for and about: Jane, my wife, Emily and Julia, my grand-daughters, and all my friends who are kind enough to read this madness.

Acknowledgments

I'd like to thank my high school English teacher for being so complimentary of my writing abilities. She made me want to continue being a writer.

Also, I must thank Bob Hackett for being the first person I ever met who kept a journal and encouraging me to do the same. He was a cool guy and made writing seem like a worthwhile endeavor.

Song lyrics are a form of poetry I have come to love, so I'd also like to thank all my buddies who wrote songs with me: Pierre Grill of Rendezvous Studios, Jerry Steelfox, John Morris, Gyula Schrieber, Jim Erhart, Gabe Preis, Jojo Russell, "Rabbit" Mackay, Chris Woods, Barba Rosa, Antonio Azevedo, and Davo.

And finally, I'd like to thank my loving wife, Jane Smith-Martin for thirty-seven wonderful years of marriage, for being supportive of my writing and telling me I could spend some more money to publish this, my second book of poetry madness. I hope you enjoy this collection and may it inspire you to write some.

Table of Contents

WITH ME ALWAYS

If ever you feel discouraged

Or find yourself the least bit forlorn

Remember that I have loved you

Even before you were born

And I will always love you

Even when we're apart

I'll carry you with me always

Safe, right here in my heart.

JUST A LOOK

You inspire me

Never tire me

Give me giggles

Bounce my knee

Little Ms. Wiggles

Don't you see?

The joy you bring

Comes back to you

In songs I sing

And every time you look my way

You brighten up my cloudy day

I should write this in a book

You lighten my heart with just a look

JANUARY 21, 2006

Emily Jade is just four months old

and in this brief span of time on earth

has acquired quite a few names; truth be told:

There's Sugar Plum, Baby Boo, We are so in love with you.

Hugger Buns, Sweetie Pie, You're the apple of our eyes.

Lover Bug, Smiley face, How you brighten up the place.

Poopy Pants, Thunder Butt, Piss and Poop and Power Futt.

Big Eyes, Bright Eyes, Where'd you get those Thunder Thighs?

Caterpillar, Sweeter Bee, Prettiest little thing I ever did see.

Fusser Butt, Or Sleepy Head, Are you going to go to bed?

Snuggle Love, Our sweet Emi, Wrapped up like a Musubi.

Sleeper Peep, Futt Button, You're so cute just doing nothin'.

Cuddle Kitten, Bing Bing, Loves to hear her daddy sing.

Little Lizard, Snuggle love, Sweeter Beater, Wuub Wuub.

Curly Girlie, Blue Berry, Little Monkey, Ears so hairy.

Snuggle Buns, Miss M.J., Bubble Girl, Who loves to play.

Swee Pee, Mung Mung, Bubblelicious, Precious one.

Booga Booga, Munchkin, Sweeper Peep, Say, how you been?

Miss Bubbles, Schnub Bub, Emmer loves a tummy rub.

Call her all you like, She won't come.

It's not because she's deaf or dumb.

She'd rather rest and suck her thumb.

Besides, she's too young to walk or run,

That's all.

Can't even crawl,

But isn't she a baby doll?

A CHEERFUL HEART

Let me tell you 'bout this baby-child

The one I know who loves to smile

It's like Happiness is her middle name

And a cheerful heart, her claim to fame

She sings, she shouts, she looks about

Baby talk and body language

And a smile that melts like butter

There is no other to compare

And I can't help but smile whenever Emily is there

THROUGH BABY'S EYES

Oh, to see the world
Through a baby's eyes
The wonder, the joy
And silent surprise

To burst into laughter
Jump for joy
Entertained by just living
Not a game or toy

When everything's still a mystery
And so many things are new
All is comfort and cuddles
And the world revolves around you.

WISHIN'

Life is but a wishing well

Praying for a penny

And if you don't have any

You can still wish as well

I won't tell

Dreams aren't made of money

Every smile is free

I am a wealthy man whenever you're with me

I wish that we'll always be

I love to watch you as you grow

And wrote these words to let you know

YOUR FIRST ULTRASOUND

Don't take it as an insult
I don't mean to put you down
But the very first time I saw you in your first ultra-sound
You looked like a little lizard to me
But that's not what you turned out to be
Not you, with those baby blues and chubby cheeks
And you've grown a lot in a few short weeks

I love that your mommy brings you over
To see us once in a while
You've captured my heart with your cute little yawns
And that adorable baby smile

I'll walk you when you're fussy
And hold you while you sleep
And though I have to give you back
I wish you were mine to keep
You brighten up my whole world
I'm so happy when you're near
Welcome to life in paradisc
I'm so glad that you are here.

CAN'T BEAT THE BEATLES

Koo Koo Ka Chew

  Where's the walrus?

Na Na Na Nice to Let It Be

  Be Be Be the Beatles

(shoot me) Set me free

  Lady in da Diamond Sky

So many "Wonder Whys" in the music I knew

  Wondering as I grew

What's with that Koo Koo Ka Chew?

  Why's there an Eggman?

No one I think is in my tree,

  Oblada, Obladee

Most every kid's a wanna-be

  Wanna be the Beatles

Wanna wear long hair

  And all's fair in Love and Peace

Or all we're just saying is to give it a chance or

  You may be a lover but you ain't no dance-sir

And in the end, we were taught to sing,

  The love you take… is equal to the love… you make.

STRICTLY PROSE

No Poetry.

    No Siree,

        Not a rhyming word or sound

            around here, my dear

Strictly prose for those who knows

    No poetry, and as for me

        To quote a man of means,

A poem can say more than it seems.

If the sound of words disturb your ear

    With muffled meanings quite unclear,

        To romp, to roam, to laugh and play

    With so much more or less than words can say.

Sunshine's Gold across the cloudless Blues

    Take no offense, now gents,

        that's just the sort of thing we poets do.

THIS MYSTERY

Life can be a mystery, a puzzle we cannot see

A maze we wander through, wondering what to do.

Joy and pain. Sun and rain

Faith and hope. Courage to cope

Dreams and plans and "I don't understands."

Life is full of ups and downs, smiles and frowns

Love and loss, dental and mental floss

Singing and dancing, heart-felt romancing

Laughter and tears, hopes and fears

Learning and yearning, building and burning

Sickness and health, tight times and wealth

Struggles and strife, this journey through life

All that we need, to grow, to love, to succeed

But we only have one, so let's strive to have fun.

Texter's Lament

Now I lay me down to text.

    I have no idea what happens next.

My thumbs keep tapping, without rest,

    My phone, the portal to this digital quest.

Who to message? What to say?

    I find my mind in complete disarray.

I scroll and scroll, my thumbs start to ache,

    But still, I can't seem to take a break.

Connection is key, but so is rest,

    And I can't let this small device control my best.

And if I wake up to see the light,

    I'll know that I made it through the night.

But if I should die before this is sent,

    I hope someone wonders where I went.

MY MARVELOUS MOTHER

Mom, I think you're fantastic, fabulous and fun,

fondly affectionate and amazingly awesome

You're comforting, caring and kind,

the apple of our eyes, warm, witty and wise

You light up our lives like a morning sunrise

Our guiding light, both beautiful and bright,

Your love's a shelter in our life's storm,

You keep us safe and warm

You're gentle, genuine, and generous

Glorious and great, devoted and dependable

Humorous yet humble… unforgettable

You're tremendously tender,

Truthful and trustworthy

Selfless and sweet, you make our lives complete

Optimistic and excellent, neighborly and nice

You are a hard-working woman

Who is elegant and graceful, joyful and playful

You're faithful, forgiving and fun-loving

Yes, you are reliable and righteous,

A child of God

Cheerful and charming, lovely and loving

You are always Understanding,

Upstanding, and Outstanding

My marvelous Mom

FIND JOY

Buy it, use it, break it, lose it. We consumers, we must choose it.

From phones to cars to candy bars.

We are eating, talking, driving.

We'll do anything to keep surviving.

Change it, rearrange it. Can't face it? Best erase it.

Computers, TVs, and other machines;

we rely on them more and more it seems.

Scrunch it, scoot it, better reboot it.

When technology fails, we still pursue it

Use your imagination to improve your situation.

Creativity can lead to innovation.

Don't succumb to the daily grind.

Find joy in each day and peace of mind.

Our legacy is not in our possessions.

It's in the memories of our life's sessions

Life is short; tell everyone, have some fun until it's done.

Emily's Senior Prom Poem

As the stars above shine bright,

We seniors gather in delight,

Dressed in our coolest duds,

To celebrate and dance with our buds.

Friends hug and laugh with glee,

Memories shared for all to see,

The music flows loud and clear.

And we're so happy to be here.

Appetizers that make us drool

Delicious dinners and desserts, so cool,

The laughter echoes through the night,

Taking photos with smiles so bright

The fun never seems to end,

As we dance and laugh with friends,

The joy of our senior prom,

Will stay with us as time goes on.

THAT BENSON BOY

So full of life, a man who cares

A friend to all and that's so rare.

Surfing the net, always on the go

With a mind so quick, he always knows

What's new, what's hot, what's what and what's not.

A wealth of knowledge and advice that's sound

Helping us all to rise, never putting us down

With a spirit so bold, and a heart so bright,

Sometimes he's wrong, but more often he's right

And so he reminds us as you might have guessed

"Appreciate all life brings and always stay blest."

WHERE HATRED STARTS

There is evil here

    And it didn't come from God

        Or the stars

            Or the earth and sky

It's not from Satan's power

            And here's the reason why

Let me tell you

    Where hatred starts

            In human hearts

            Human hearts

SABBATHS

Some say
  every day
    should be God's day

I think each breath is enough ritual
        Each sunrise enough hope

        So, I don't set my sights
                on a heaven far
or save every wish for night's first star

Since I live my life with nothing to fear
        And my heart reminds me that heaven,
              Like God,
                    Is here.

TWO WORDS

If anyone should ever ask me…

    (and they haven't)

        to condense the Bible

to make it super simple

      so everyone can understand

    I would write just one page

      So it could be on billboards, posters, t-shirts

One page with just two words: Be good

I figure if you're looking for good, bad takes a backseat

And what is "good?"

        Let your heart tell you.

FOR JANE

I wrote this poem

This night to say

You are my light

My light of day

Don't ever take your light

Your love, away

I Fall Hard

In our alone positive vibrations paradise

When each and every moment rises way beyond

That's so good or this is nice

Such good feelings abound and surround us

As we pursue nature's needs

With astonishing results

I drink in your loving eyes

With unquenchable thirst

You, the last and the first, Island girl

Of the rest of my life

Intrigued and absolutely crazy about you

For when I fall, I fall hard

So glad to be

So toe-tingling happy

In this and every moment

By your side

JONESIN' FOR JANIE

Addicted to your love

Gotta have you

For the comfort of your company

Need to hold you

To taste that tenderness

Want to sleep beside you

Since I've built my dreams around you

Must tell you

All my thoughts and hopes and fears

I go into withdrawal when you work late

Or take travel trips

Or get upset with me

Get the shakes

When I sense your passion

Want you more and more

Happy to overdose on affection

Content in my addiction to your love

I Can Never Hear That Too Much

Imagine me

Deck-side

Wind-blown

Home

And she shouts

"I love my house

and I love my spouse!

Wow

I can never hear that too much

Life's not tough, it's sweet

Forget the heat

Lounge in the love

This is my life

Here with my darling

My wife

POEM WAITING

There's a poem waiting
In your willing heart

Hidden between the words
So as not to offend

Immersed in metaphor mayhem
To bring out a smile

Wrapped up in the love of syntax and syllables
The magic of language

Smothered in love like simile pancakes
in thick maple syrup

For you, always for you

There's a love poem in here somewhere

THE SECRET

Lucky me…
I've found the secret
To a wonderful life:
Marry the right woman

There's nothing like
A working wife

Life can be sweet
Sometimes it's rough
But life with you, darling?
I can never get enough.

Janie, you're my world
My stars
My sun
Now, as always
You are my only one

SIX DEER

Six deer

    Just walked by here

On their breakfast hike

    Which I hope they like

White tail flags a-flyin'

    Tryin' to be invisible amongst the trees

These deer now know

They are welcome here

    To tread the leaves and snow

SOMEDAY

Someday

I'll understand it all

Or at least more

If not enough

It's tough being ignorant

Of life

Of eternity

Faith has its pitfalls and challenges

Its questions

Devine guidance

It's a happy ending story

When tears will cease

And death will be no more

And all God's children say "Amen"

And line up at the door

SURROUNDED

Happiness has me surrounded, has all of my life, mostly

So lucky to have had two loving parents

And a wonderful family now

With a loving wife, three great kids

And two darling grand-daughters

My life's hurts have been few

A broken heart or two, some pulled muscles

But I've had great adventures on land and sea

Meaningful work teaching and artistic creations

Our own home in an island paradise

Like a botanical garden landscape on a mountainside

We've got rainbows and sun showers

Music and laughter, faith and fun

Yes, I am one lucky son of a gun

RAY-SHAW-FLAY

At breakfast today

Over reshuffle

I had the pleasure to dine

With a new friend of mine

A scruffy fox

He crunched away

On frozen crab cakes

And I, a bagel with cheese

It's moments like these

That I commune with cute critters

Outside my warm home window

With his footprints in freshly fallen snow

A new friend

I am now happy to know

LOOKING FOR ANSWERS

I have a good question:

How can I best serve God?

Wish I knew the answer.

Wonder if I can do it?

If I figure out what it is, will I do it?

Will it be fun?

Will it help others or myself or both?

Will it be a life-long mission

or a small favor?

A one-time assignment

A gig. A challenge.

An adventure! A quest! Yes!

If only I had a burning bush

Or divine E-mail

Angelic visitation would suffice

It'd sure be nice to know what God wants

If God wants anything at all

A SINGING SOUL

Having learned laughter early on

And heard the world wake at dawn

And found that love can give us wings

My soul sings

Having tasted wealth over time

prefer water over wine

Life's misfits are friends of mine

My soul sings

Knowing life is short, the fun of play

How good it is to give away to those in need

My needs are met and yet I yearn

To learn more and my soul sings

To see all the possibilities

Love my life; I am set free

So my soul sings

And when I die and fly as light

I'm sure it all works out alright

I won't complain or put up a fight

I'm heaven-ready. My soul sings

SMOKER'S LAMENT

I grew up next to a tobacco barn

That aroma in my young lungs

We kids rolled those leaves to make smoke bombs

We saw no harm

Just like Huck Finn, I made me a corn cob pipe

And started a journey of smokin' and chockin'

For most of my life

Puffin' on a pipe sure burns your tongue

But I was dumb when I was young

I thought life's about lookin' for fun: ya gotta grab it

And I got plenty of time to break any nasty habit

Then along came cigarettes; they seemed easier somehow

I just wish I knew then what I know now

That demon Nicotine wouldn't leave me alone

And I ended up startin' to roll my own

I never chewed it, didn't vape it

Quit lots of times but couldn't escape it

Then one fateful morn I couldn't catch my breath

Take me to the hospital; this is scaring me to death

The doctors all told me, "You shouldn't smoke."

Now I've done it, my heart is broke.

My veins are clogged, there's fluid in my lungs

I thought I was invincible when I was young

Smoking never helped me, not one bit

Nearly dying did, 'cause finally I've quit

REACHING FOR STARS

Eccentric artist,
  paints his mind.

Adventurous rebel,
  breaks the rules.

Thoughtful philosopher,
  ponders life.

Free-spirited dreamer,
  reaches for the stars.

Determined fighter,
  never gives up.

  Don't laugh
I'm busy carving my own path.

FOR YOU HONEY

Honey, I love the touch of you

And can never get too much of you

I enjoy your company

And every moment you're close to me

I like your looks, your laugh, your smile

And just to get alone with you for a while

I like the way you act when you're around me

And thank my lucky stars for the day you found me

I hope this is just the beginning, just the start

I give you my dreams, my love, my heart

I'M YOURS

Slow dance

    Perchance this is my lucky night

You, here in my arms

Feeling so right

    Holding me tight

Turn down the light

    Just you and I and the radio

    Taking it slow

I'm yours and it shows

    Oh, those special secrets no one else knows

    Sweet romance

But for now, let's just dance.

CITY SIGHTS

It's a Cadillac

Kitty Kat

Let me take you for a ride in the back

Or cruise the strip and you can strut your stuff

You are too much

I can't get enough

Trust me honey, ain't no line

And would you prefer your place or mine?

A Home Poem

There should be a poem here

Somewhere

A home to rest your head

A stove, a bed

To eat and sleep

To laugh and weep

The many things a home can be

With you

For me

A place we can be free

Full of flowers

Up streams

Under trees

Time to do as we please

Some work or play

You pick the day

We could adventure or roam

But I prefer… home

NEW VOWS

I vow to keep on loving you.

    I will support your interests.

        I will always forgive you.

I'll always be happy to hug and to hold you.

    I will be sure to check with you

        about all our life's big decisions.

I will do my best to keep laughter in our lives.

    I will respect your beliefs

        though they may differ from my own.

I will drive you places if you want me to.

    I will strive to be understanding

        and respect your opinions.

It's OK to have time apart and different interests.

    You make me feel like a wealthy man.

        You are my cuddle kitten and my muse.

I would love to travel the world with you.

      I love you from your ears to your nose,

        your knees to your toes

and all those parts of marvelous you.

You are my light, the one who makes everything right,

      I delight in my marvelous you,

      Your presence, your patience are pleasures I treasure

Make of me the story of your life.

            And I thank you for being my wife.

Journaling With Jesus

Lord you know me,

      even the number of hairs on my head

         You know my true self and yet forgive my faults

      I am encouraged by Your love

but disappointed by my inability to live up to my faith

         I'm full of questions, selfish in my desires

You've given me many talents

      yet even my way with words leaves me numb,

            strikes me dumb

      I'm in awe of what I could be

         If I was more like you and less like me

You know how my story ends

      I know only that it depends,

         depends on the choices I make

My desire to avoid making mistakes

I want to hear your voice.

    Guide me to each thoughtful choice.

Help me learn to listen.

    I am fearful of the silence,

        Scared of what you may require of me

Your Holy Spirit convicts me

    though that's just what I need

But if there's a cross to bear, just like your son,

    I'd rather not bleed.

I have no prophesies to fulfill

    No punishment should I sidestep Your will

Plenty of excuses but nothing sticks.

    You know all my tricks.

I hope sometimes I make you laugh.

Please put in a good word to God on my behalf.

COVID COMMENTARY

Long story short

    It seems some scientific

Secret recipe pandemic pancakes

    Have brought us a breakfast of champions

    Yea! Hey! We all stay home!

And we might benefit

    From just being alone

    Because now we realize

        How blessed it can be

        To socialize

MARIJAHOOJIE

Find it

Grind it

Poke it

Smoke it

Take it easy

Toke it easy

Don't cough

Your head off

Medicine of mayhem

Altered consciousness

Reality break

I pray the Lord my soul to bake

NO FILTER

Us independent thinker stinkers

Speak without censure

Say whatever floats our boat

Even if it gets your goat

All in good fun

And when it's done…

No Hun, it's not over

We relish this moment now

Celebrate life's moments of "Wow!"

And when the lights go down

We're gonna party here

So send in the clowns

And pass out the beer

THE 1921 TULSA MASSACRE

Man's inhumanity to man
Is a fire burning Black lives
The hopes and homes
Of the black side of Tulsa
Leaving cinders of memories
Burnt into the brains of black children
Cringing in fear amid the bullets and bombs
What is going on?
Why are they killing the black folks?
Finding no shelter
even in the shadow of the cross
So much was lost
And yet they rebuilt
Reclaimed their part of town
That's what true survivors do
When hateful fools try to burn everything down

A MIND OF ITS OWN

My mind at times has a mind of its own

And it won't leave me alone

Keeps on yackin' in my head

Instead of meditatin' or contemplatin' peacefully

It won't let me be

Has got so much to say and won't go away

How does one run from oneself

In which direction of introspection can I flee

If I am never rid of me?

I take me with me wherever I go

And I know it's nuts, no ifs or ands or buts

I'm whack and a filter, I lack

So I just say what I please when I shoot the breeze

And at times like these it seems the thing to do

So what bruddah, boddah you?

GOT A LETTER

I got a letter from God

I swear, addressed to me

    And signed by the Almighty

It began:

        Dear Rod

            Dear child of God

I hope this letter finds you well

    With lots of tales of joy to tell

This is just a brief note to say

    May you be blessed and centered

        (Most of the day)

            May love guide your way

    Please share all you can

And be a good man.

        The Almighty

The Church of Inquiring Christians

Love first. Love wins.

Love gives life meaning, purpose and joy.

If you learn but one thing in this life, learn to love

It's OK to debate or question everything

Everything we're told about God

Your Spiritual/Religious beliefs are your own

And are most likely unlike anyone else's.

Make a list of questions you'd like to ask God.

Like why mosquitos?

Everyone's welcome here.

Diversity breeds contentment.

One of our rules is there are no enforceable rules.

Church attendance is encouraged but not required.

You can Zoom it, phone it in or leave a text message.

There will be no collection plates passed around

Though a donation box should be available

There are no papers to sign. No oaths.

No rituals other than baptism.

Funerals will be called Celebrations of One's Life.

Dogma is discouraged but pets are allowed.

Anger, hatred, racism, and cruelty are not allowed.

Church recreational activities: Field trips, picnics, hiking, biking, swimming, and boating.

Suggestions entertained.

There are no preachers, just congregational sharing, guest speakers, occasional videos or visiting choirs or musicians.

Have fun with your spiritual experience and share it freely with anyone who is interested in knowing more about it.

No one knows the mind of God but let's hope he's in a good mood when we meet him or her.

Remember your faith when you eat or drink.

Grace is optional but quite OK.

Snacks during gatherings are welcomed

but clean up after yourselves.

It's ok to pray together and anyone who has something to share should be allowed a chance to speak however, it's better to pray alone silently in a peaceful place like out in nature or in the privacy of your own room.

The Church of the Inquiring Christians is always open to suggestions on ways to improve the worship experience.

THIS RACE WITH TIME

Tick-tock, the seconds fly, I'm in this race, a race with time,

To seize the moments, make them mine.

So swiftly do the days unfold, as if a story yet untold

I stumble, fall, then rise again,

Begging for just a few moments more and then…

Bang! Goes the gun and I'm off at a run

Chasing each moment, racing each moment

These seconds slip through my fingers, swift as air

No time to mourn them, no time to spare.

With each step we take, we ache, we tire,

Life's burning desire becomes a raging fire

Embrace the rhythm, embrace the flow,

In this race with time we come to know,

That life's true meaning lies not in the chase,

But in the grace we might find at our own pace.

SO MANY WAYS TO LOVE YOU

I want to love you like a wave

that never stops crashing upon the shore

Endlessly coming back for more

To love you like a song

that sticks in my head and never fades away

A melody that lifts your spirits, whatever comes what may

I want to love you like a painting

A masterpiece that takes your breath away

A work of art that you could stare at all day

I want to love you like a memory

That lingers on, so clear and strong

A recollection that lasts all life long

I want to love you with an unending devotion,

Not just for a moment, but for an eternity unbroken.

Like the gradual melting of glaciers, a patient pace,

Or the birth of galaxies in the vastness of space.

I want to love you with a fervor uncontained,
Like laughter that bursts forth, joy unrestrained.

A love that truly matters, beyond mere perception,
A love that borders on complete perfection.

To love you like none have loved you before,
With everything I am, all that and more.
So let me love you, in all these ways
Through all the moments and all the days
Let me love you, my love, fierce and true
Yes, I promise, I will always, always love you.

EVERYTHING, EVERYWHERE, ALL AT ONCE

If there truly is a multiverse

and if that is a multitude of universes made up of every decision

a person could ever have made

that would set them on a different path

and completely change their life's circumstances

And if

EVERYTHING

is possible in this world of ours,

(though there obviously are some limitations to what is possible)

but for the sake of "Movie Magic" one is capable

of letting one's imagination run wild

and capturing it on film,

we just might find the cinematic characters

doing all kinds of strange things

running a laundry business or saving the world

while ending up

EVERYWHERE

their dreams could take them

whether it be Kung Fu Fighting in the offices of the IRS

or stranded on a lifeless planet

as two conscious pet rocks that can communicate telepathically

and move without feet

ALL AT ONCE

we amateur film critics may come to realize

if we can look beyond the flashy special effects

to see the dynamics of family relationships

and appreciate the hopes, the fears, the pain and disappointments

that make up all our lives

then we might realize that the only thing that matters

even when it seems that nothing matters

is the LOVE that can save us all.

EMA-LITA-BITA (EMILY)

Time has gone by so fast
     Wasn't it only yesterday
        that I bounced you to sleep on my knee?
And now you've grown so tall (thank God) and so smart.

I've always known you were talented,
From the first time you sang You Are My Sunshine for us
and went on to prove yourself a true professional
when you recorded Two Little Hands at Pierre's studio
with Julia as your back-up singer.

And then you went on to become an actress in show after show.
May you always enjoy the fun drama can bring.

And imagine my surprise and pride when you decided
        To become "A Teacher"
     Such a noble and rewarding occupation.

And to watch you excel in your studies: a math wiz!

How happy I was to learn you were involved in school activities

dedicated to making a difference.

Imagine my joy to learn

you were part of a group called Valedictorians!

I told you, you were smart.

And now I can brag that my first granddaughter

has earned an academic scholarship

to the University of Hawaii!

I'm happy to know you won't be far away

(Until you choose a semester abroad)

And if those college boys give you any trouble,

Just tell them your Baba has a baseball bat

And he's not afraid to use it.

You're all grown up now so I can't tell you what do

but I'm sure you'll make good decisions for yourself.

May you find great friends and have good times
and don't forget that I will always love you
and want the best for you.

You have made me so proud.

With lots of love,

Bapa

Sunday, May 30th, 2021

THIS MEMORIAL DAY

This Memorial Day
> Let us say
>> We will study war no more
In peace and play
> We will seek a way to get along
To learn how we all belong
And for the first time
> In all time
> All of us can shine the light of love
Grateful to God above
> Compassion's flame
>> In Jesus' name, Amen.

THE IMPORTANCE OF LOVE

Love makes life grand

Love wins, puts hate to shame

Love is the answer to so many of life's questions

Love is worth all the aggravation, worry or sorrow

Love can only be given, not taken

Love can be and should be fun

Love is what God wants from us

Love lasts

Love is all around us, in music and nature

In our hopes and prayers and children

Love is everlasting and kind, forgiving and patient

Love keeps no records of wrongs, holds no grudges

Love listens to the stories of others

Love is a promise of peace, trust and comfort on earth

Love is amazing

"I WANNA LOVE YOU"

I wanna love you for as long as it takes

to count all the stars in the sky

As long as it takes 'til pigs fly

I wanna love you hard like a diamond in the rough

Like a full moon sky and still that's not enough

I wanna love you like a hustler loves the game

Like Hoiudini loved his chains

Like a fire uncontained

I wanna love you crazy like a patient off their meds

Like the voices in my head

And the monsters beneath the bed. Crazy

I wanna love you like the earth after a rain

Like jumping out of a plane

Eat you up like a luscious last piece of cake

Like grilled onions and steak

A hunger I will not fake

I wanna love you like flowers in the morning

Like the rain when it starts pouring

Like the beach in the afternoon

The sun, the stars, the moon

And I don't care where or why or how

I just wanna love you now

THANKS DON

In March of 2020, Dan Lanzettle from Archer Methodist

Died of Covid 19

The newly arrived pandemic.

His death was a serious wake-up call for us all

Of trouble to come.

Woe to the elderly and those with pre-existing complications

The immune deficient or feeble

Being in the wrong place at the wrong time

Breathing the wrong air, it didn't seem fair

Was it human error?

Bat blood, bad blood

Carelessly caught then spread

Until the powers that be said, "Stay home!"

Keep your distance

Wear a mask in public 'cause there's a virus about

We still don't understand it, can't figure it out, and can't stop it

We can only slow things down

If we can only give up gathering, hugging, singing

Say goodbye to concerts and plays, sports and bars

Weddings and even family Thanksgiving

We strive to keep on living

Most will do as asked: it's only a mask

It's just all that time alone trying to entertain ourselves

If not on the phone or zoom sessions

Alone, restricted, new rules and fines

I've seen hospitals overflow

And know why there are refrigerated trucks to hold the remains

It's a numbers game we can't seem to win

As more get sick and some die

The numbers continue to rise

And still some people can't seem to realize

That something must be done

It takes everyone doing what they can

Surely that's not impossible to understand?

And when the vaccines arrive, we can go back to just being alive

Being with others, able to hug and hold, comfort and kiss

To gather again like we love to do

Until the next germ arrives and we will again risk our lives

JANUARY 6TH CAPITAL INSURRECTION

We have done wrong

Some trespassed where they don't belong

Insurrection over an election

Bringing harm

Spreading alarm

Yet we as a nation prevail

Voices of decent will be quieted

Their cause to no avail

And we will go on

With faith like our fathers for a brighter dawn

Our chance to shine

Light the lamp of liberty

To last 'til the end of time

DEAR DEER

Momma Deer

Papa Deer

Baby Deer

Bombardier

Bapa Dear

Darlin' Dear

Dis Deer

Dat Deer

These four deer

Came to breakfast here

Bringing with them a gift of poetry

This poem here

Thanks deer

<u>SCARS</u>

Got some scars

Some you can't see

Scars that are inside of me

Scars from the time someone said

"You can't love. Your heart is dead."

Scars from lies

Scars from pain

Tears and fears of being insane

Scars from words that cut me deep

Made me doubt

Disturbed my sleep

But I can handle how hurt makes me feel

I am strong

Scars show I can heal

Staying Connected With Love

You are there and I am here but daily your voice I hear

This everyday connection reflects our affection

Hooray for cell phones zooming over time zones

Even though miles apart, you have my heart

Lots of text messages, bitmoji images

Lots of hearts, full of love, all from my lover dove

Your love is all around me, via technology

Even better when it's Facetime, just to see my darling mine

If only I could touch you, to hold you and give you a kiss

This is what I miss

Romantic recycled cards in the mail,

Love them, they never get stale

Flat rate boxes full of surprise, Archer Church merchandise

Odds and ends, lots of treasure, opening up gives me pleasure

This huggerboo of mine shows his love in countless ways

Oh, to be in your arms, I can't wait for those days.

by Jane Smith-Martin

My Favorite Drug

My favorite drug

Isn't a drug at all really

I get high off of music

Melody with Harmony

Works for me

I love to make it

Or simply take it; easy listening

Enjoying the songs of others

While My Guitar Gently Weeps

Thank you George

Bless you John

Keep going Paul

Keep that beat Ringo

Take us there

With more music to spare

So kind of you to share

REQUIEM FOR TIM

Brother Tim

We will miss him

What a character

Jokester

Tripster with tales to tell

Bound for Heaven

Too weird for Hell

Upon his celestial elevation

He'll begin his cultivation

Beyond earth's imagination

Ganja strains

To amuse our brains

Keep those Pearly Gates open

Like our minds

See you…in time

NO FILTER

I say what I please

But please don't take offense

From words such as these

I mean you no harm

I just like to play

And it's hard to stay silent

When there's just so much to say

IF ONLY ROD WAS HERE

The Great Conjunction, Jupiter and Saturn

What a sight, this winter solstice night

We had to witness this event, this once-in-a-lifetime wonder

With family members, Emily, Julia, Sam and Jen

Even Betty, Holly and Ed joined in then

So with laughter, fun and sharing, so nice to gather once again

To be together with loved ones dear

Ah, if only Rod was here

As positive numbers soar, no browsing craft fairs and stores

Pandemic distractions, worldwide infection and death

What a mess this virus has been and it's not over yet

Will we ever return to normal, come and go as we please?

Will mankind ever contain this disease?

It's scary, don't panic, ganbatte, take a stand

I need somebody to hold my hand

Ah, if only Rod was here

Lonely nights, a too-quiet house

'tis hard to rouse a Yuletide cheer

The home-made wreaths are up, along with twinkling lights

Christmas is coming I remind myself

With only me, myself and I, we manage to get by

To work and keep up this paradise estate

What's missing is my mate

Ah, if only Rod was here

But wait

He is here

Here in my heart

By Jane Smith-Martin

Things I Don't Want, and Do

I don't want to believe in the devil
I consider him to be a scapegoat
We can blame our evil thoughts and actions on

I don't want to follow a vengeful God
Who would say "I am sick of man" and then flood the world
And drown his children like rats
A jealous God who when he saw us worshipping idols
Told the Israelites to kill every man, woman, child and goat
And then take their land for themselves

I reject a God who would rain down fire
To kill his own children should they displease Him

I want to believe in a loving God
Who sent his son, Jesus to teach us to care
To love Him and each other

For Love is the most wonderful force for good

In this entire universe

I want to believe we are God's children,

capable of living forever

I know I have much to learn

But I am free to believe what I choose

And I choose to believe in the power of love

God is Love and Love wins

Tears will cease

Hatred and pain will be no more

We will put an end to war

And let love lead us to be compassionate beings

Able to reinvent the world for good

Forever

For I ask this in Jesus name,

Amen.

IRONY

I came home to keep Mom alive

Reunited with my church

And make it my business to seek out the shut-ins

To help get them out to church

And then a virus arrived as if to say, "Stay home!"

And it seemed ironic, almost funny

Until friends started dying

Not much fun in that

And where am I now?

At home

We all stay home

Yes, I stay home, missing my other home

My life

My darling

My wife

In Memory of Win Lampert, Poet

Good

Better

Best

Never let it rest

'Til the good

Is better

And the better…

Best

COME FILL ME

And empty cup I be

Asking kindly, Lord, come fill me

Enjoy life in my shell

Tell me when I'm doing well

Lead me to where I can be of service

I'm rusty at prayer and just a little bit nervous

Devine driver, take my soul for a spin

Forgive me those 'never dones'

And oh so many "should have beens'

I'm just a vessel, cracked and worn

A flag flown too long, now faded and torn

But since the day I was born, it has served me well

Here between heaven and hell

Night and day, rest and play

Hope and despair, I keep breathing air

Keep on plugging away

So come on, help me see

Replenish the light in me

And let's seize the day

FOR MOM MARTIN

In this season of giving I just want to say

You have given me more than I can ever repay

As a small boy, you watched over me

And as a young man you let me be free

I want so much to thank you

For guiding and providing, prodding, protecting

Helping and healing, playing and staying

Hugging and holding, the occasional scolding

Wanting the best for me, forgiving the rest for me

A mother who cares just by being there

You mean so much to me and I will always be in your debt

I hope I never forget all the love and fun

All those things you've done to make my life fine

The tears and the time, darling mother mine

I can never repay, I'm just trying to say

That I love you so and though I know that you know

It's worth saying again and again

Can I get an "Amen"?

Questions for Education

Can we prepare our students for a nuclear-free future?

What can we teach them about love?

What ecological lessons best suit our global warming classrooms?

Where do we stand on the fate of man?

Do we teach the pursuit of happiness or what freedom means?

Must they only read and compute or can they create and dream?

Do we celebrate the diversity of cultures or sing my country, right or wrong?

Dare we teach the peace of meditation or the sense of oneness of being out in nature?

Is History to be found in a list of wars and battles or a compilation of our art and music, discoveries and accomplishments?

Can they save for the future, balance a budget and spend wisely?

Do we box them in or show them how to think outside the box?

Can we lead them to clear, logical, tolerant, global thinking?

Are we preparing them not to be fooled or manipulated?

Do we teach them how food can be their medicine?

Do we teach them to deal with stress, depression and alienation?

Have they learned to listen to one another and share fairly in conversation?

Have we found ways to make our lessons fun and interesting?

Do they respect others, question authority, laugh, sing and play?

Are we preparing them for the world of the future?

Are we helping them or boring them?

Is it our place to teach them the importance of forgiveness?

Are we molding them into submissive citizens?

Do we just want them to sit down and be quite or is it Ok to question the relevance of our lessons?

Is it appropriate to discuss terrorism, abuse, greed and hatred?

Shall we warn them about the military-industrial complex?

Should we encourage them to serve in the military or avoid war at all costs?

Are they too young or are we too late?

Who will care for us in times to come, heal our hurts, sculpt our gardens, write our novels, protect our wilderness, care for our ocean, and find new solutions?

What kind of world are we leaving for these children?

Now that we can communicate faster and farther, have we found anything meaningful to say?

Are we asking the right questions?

What is our plan?

Who gets to decide?

Do we know what we're doing?

Are we doing no harm?

Two P-R-I-S-O-N Poems

Put away, out of sight, out of mind

Rights? You've got to be kidding

Insane people, angry dudes, sad sorts

So much time with so little to do

Only a number

No one knows what it's like

Paying societal dues

Really would rather be anywhere else

Isolated from friends and family

Sad sometimes beyond hope

Oh, how I miss my life

Now it's just time after time

I WAS MADE FOR POETRY

My body is like a poem

It seems it's full of rhymes

That's what I've noticed

So many, many times

See, I have toes, a chin and nose

Cheeks and lips, arms and hips

Shoulders, thighs

Brows over my eyes

Fingers, thumbs and eardrums

My throat and breast

My hairy chest

My teeth and tongue

Heart and lungs

So much of me just rhymes, you see

Like I was made for poetry

AND THE POET SANG....

Love has been around

A long, long time

Since humans first touched

Love has been through changes

Improvements

Challenges

This emotion of devotion

That person who fills my head and heart

Those moments apart

That remind me we are always together

Love is, was, will always be a good reason

To keep living

Keep learning

Keep laughing

And the poet sang:

"Yes, I know enough of love

To know love is enough for me."

THANKS

I want always to express my thanks

For the many blessings

That fill my life

My loving wife

Great kids

And granddaughters

Seems to me my whole life

Has been filled with fun and meaning

Adventure and compassion

I welcome Your return

I yearn to see the day Your will is done

Here on earth just as it is in heaven.

All this and more in Jesus name, Amen.

GOD'S PARTY

Pain free

Sin free

Free to be children of God

No tears will be shed

Folks no longer are dead

Praise through song

Where we all get along

Wash my feet

Let's provide for those

With not enough to eat

To find out what's really going on

Read Matthew,

Mark,

Luke

And John

OUR LOVE POEM TOGETHER

We've been together

    for most of our lives' good times

        learning to love each other

To support

    To share

        To be there

Where are the words to say, "Thank you"

How can I express all the joy you bring to me

    How your love has set me free

        I can be myself

            And still you love me

And that

    Is all

        I need.

I Talked to God

I talked to God today

OK- you can say I prayed

But there's more

For the first time ever

God talked back!

Now, am I whacked?

Do others hear Him too?

I know He said some stuff in the Bible

Through burning bushes

And clouds and thunder

He gave some commandments

To steer us clear of wrongdoing

But what's He doing talking to me?

"Rest easy, dear child for you are loved"

And I felt good.

Yes, this should last me for a while.

CURIOUS

I don't mean to pry

But that look in your eye

Makes me wonder "why?"

Why you bother with me?

To be friends, to spend time?

I'm just curious, what do you see in me?

Can you imagine what I'm thinking?

Does it show that I'm beginning to care?

That I'm glad you're there?

Do you see what I see?

How wonderful love can be,

If it should happen

To you

And me?

OLYMPICS

by Bapa and Emily

Humans love contests

Canada has the syrup

Hawaii has the best climate

Sox and sandals, the footwear of champions

I used to pole vault over nine feet high

But now, I race to the bottom of the pretzel bag

Marathon, Man, are they crazy?

That's gym-nasty

Stop running and start sitting

Couch potatoes to the starting cushion!

Birds of a feather watch Telly together

Indoor weather

Whether you like it or not

It's hot.

MysFyt's Lament

When Tommy's fear kept him from opening the door
The police crawled in through the kitchen window
    To answer a noise complaint call
    All six officers came to quiet a crazy kid
Who had recently been released from twelve years
    At Greystone psychiatric hospital
    Thinking he was under attack,
    Tommy opened his faithful switchblade
    His fateful mistake, creating a lethal situation
    Requiring retaliation
    Which the boys in blue would willingly supply
Without asking "Why", without so much as a word
    Eight shots were heard.
    Three different service revolvers
    Unloaded eight shots into Tommy's chest
    The rest is history, Tommy is history
    And only I remain to tell you of my pain

<u>You Can Rhyme</u>

Poetry

Can really be

Done so easily

With so many words that sound the same

It can be lots of fun, like playing a game

You can rhyme here or you can rhyme there

You can rhyme most anywhere

You can rhyme up in a tree

Whatever you say is OK with me

You can rhyme just for fun or for something to say

Some people rhyme most every which way

You can rhyme with a story you make up with a friend

With a world full of words, the fun need never end

You can rhyme high or you can rhyme low

You can take a rhyme with you wherever you go

You can rhyme in your bedroom or on your back porch

Rhyme by candlelight or lamplight

By flashlight or torch

You can rhyme for the challenge or to just pass the time

It can be silly or sassy as long as it rhymes

You can rhyme pickles with tickles

Eat steaks with snakes

Try oodles of noodles or fresh frosted flakes

Make a wish with a fish, chase a fly in the sky

Share hot dogs with bullfrogs or eat hot apple pie

You can rhyme first thing in the morning

Or on a lazy afternoon

You can turn a rhyme into a song if you can find a tune

Sing it, shout it, tell everyone about it

Let your folks know you're just working on your flow

Can a drizzle fizzle?

Does a stream dream?

You could me a poet and not even know it

Rhyming sturgeon with surgeon

Without any urgin'

Nice dreams and moonlight

Ice cream and frostbite

Nothin' to it

I know you can do it

You can razzle and dazzle until you're quite frazzled

Rhyme stuff with bluff and huff with puff

(Tell me when you've had enough)

You can rhyme at a party or rhyme when you're home

Just keep on rhyming

And you'll end up with a poem

Senior Moments

Sometimes when there's a "difficulty"

You hear people say, "Forget about it."

But when one can no longer remember

Even the simplest things, they can be quite "difficult"

Memories fade, and all those "Remember the times…?

Are answered: "Nope" it becomes obvious

When a person starts to repeat the questions

They asked not long ago,

They can't remember directions

They ask things like, "What was I doing?"

"Where are we going again?"

"Where did I put that damn phone?"

They feel frustrated and you feel sorry for them

For their loss, their memory loss

Can lead to mourning for bits of life lost

It's not dying but it must feel like checking out early

But no matter what happens

I'll always remember you, my friend

Or will I?

MY MIND

I can imagine peace

    But the world doesn't change

I can believe in God

    But never hear his or her voice

I can hope for the will to heal myself

    And still be sick

"The power of the Mind…"

I'm a fizzled-out fuse

    A rusty gate

        An old operating system

        A tube TV

My mind is not all it's cut out to be.

WHERE FREEDOM STARTS

Freedom begins within

It involves experimentation

Can be found in meditation

It can be given away

With wishes and whims

It can be taken away

With laws and iron bars

Lost or found

Look around

Really learn to see

Truly love

And that can set you free

LOVE A DOVE

When a healthy male dove

Spies a lady dove to love

He approaches her with bows

And tail feathers spread

And I clearly heard what he said

And I'll tell you now

I swear

It was, "Wow!"

NEW WAYS TO BE

When the year is new

We seem to feel we are too

We believe in possibilities

Even beyond our capabilities

And that's OK

That's how we find new ways to be

Could anyone have imagined the texts, the phones

Computer power in the palm of our hands

So much to learn, so much we don't understand

We can shape a paradise with peace on earth

Wouldn't that be nice

And if we can dream it, it could be

I only hope I live to see a better world in tranquility

Where we can all get along

Where we can sit and sing

Thankful for what the future can bring

TROUBLE IN THE WOODS

Billy Joe Bob and his buddy Zebediah

Are out hunting in the woods

When suddenly, Zebediah falls flat and twitches twice

While his eyes roll back in his head

And it looks like he isn't breathin'

Billy Joe Bob starts to panic and calls 911.

"Nine, one, one: what is your emergency?"

You gotta help me; my friend Zeb just fell down dead.

"Now, just take it easy. I can help, just follow my instructions:

First, let's make sure he's really dead"

There's a short pause and then the operator hears

A loud BANG!

Then Billy Joe Bob comes back on the line and says,

"OK, now what?"

Deceptively Addictive

Women are amazing

So complex to the point of being incomprehensible

And they're beautiful
Except when they're angry

They can be cute or cunning
Dedicated or deceptive

Alluring and addictive

Hard to live without
Or with

I'd really rather have back my rib

PASSION AND PLAY

Inspired by Jason Silva

To distill the world into words is a poet's passion and play

Join me in rewriting the human story

With images of our infinite imagination

Progressing towards the positive possibilities of existence

Consider our compassionate collective consciousness

Continually evolving and solving,

Surviving and striving to better ourselves

Harming no one, helping someone

Reveling in our insatiable optimism

As who we are becomes what we can be

Our space-age overview of Earth shows no national borderlines

Transcending tribal troubles, we migrate to integrate

Becoming enlightened manifestations of our selfless selves

Following our blissful joy layered in love

An irrefutable faith founded in awe

Serendipity and lucidity at odds with absurdity and stupidity

The mind beyond time at play in the moment

Letting go in order to grow as the unknown beckons us onward

Exploring, expanding and exploding beyond our comfort zones

There is more to us than even we allow

Beyond what's here, longer than this "Now"

This paradigm moment of mind

Emotionally eager for the oneness of art and music

Stories, songs, drama and dance

This is mankind's unintelligent design, ever wanting more

And even if all things end in rot

We should be joyful now with all we've got

All we see with all our friends, this moment now that never ends

Take that cognitive leap to something new

However strange, fear not the change in you

Embrace the wondrous possibility of what change can do.

PREPARE A PLACE

Jesus said,

"I go to prepare a place for you."

My earthly dad said,

"I go to warn God about you,

I hope you get in."

I said, "It's about where you're going,

Not just where you've been"

My sweet mother said,

"Heaven help us all."

HYPOTHETICALS

My friend and I love to talk about God

He doubts and I believe

We laugh and tease and bounce around in hypotheticals

Could be's and can't be's

Eternal life and Ain't gonna happen

We occasionally agree

I stand fast and he scores points off me

I hope for pearly gates

But when I ask him what he thinks awaits,

He says, "Just nothing."

No consciousness?

No continuity?

Dead in a box?

I must admit such a philosophy

makes this one line seem special

Because it ends, friends.

Yet it all depends on one's faith
I'm hoping I'm eternal
 and will eventually get used to it forever
The possibilities would be, could be endless
Though hard to prove

You don't know until you go
And that's alright with me
The hope of heaven awaits and that too, sets me free
And if nothingness awaits, I won't complain
No, I won't care. Without my spirit, my soul, I'm nowhere
Without my Lord, without love, I'd already be gone
But thanks to faith, I'm happy to carry on
Yes, I've got questions, doubts too
I've felt righteous and endured the blues
But I'll tell you what I know in my heart to be true
Jesus had me at, "Love God and your neighbors too."

WRITTEN FOR JANE

during a Kayak Trip

(On the North Shore of the Big Island)

In my quiet times of reflection
My thoughts fly to you
Like birds seeking the shelter
Of the evening's Banyan tree

I send with them
All my love
And hope for your happiness
And just a touch of missing
Until I'm kissing you again

CHEERS

Crash and burn

The car turns over and over

A circle of flame and flashing steel

"Hey guys, look how much I can drink."

"Hey world, look how fast I can drive"

And when the beer spilled

Off the dash and into my lap

In that moment of distraction

The slowed speed of my reaction

As I crossed over the double line

Into the oncoming lights

"Hey heaven, see how fast my young spirit soars

Above the flaming wreck

That contains a broken and mangled vehicle

My souls chariot

My charred body

Cheers

THAT AMAZING JULIA

She's a firecracker, a burst of light

Her imagination soars in flight

Her talents are endless, her energy too

Our world awaits all she will do

Her drawings are masterpieces, works of art

Each stroke of the pencil, a beat of her heart

Her sketches come to life, living stories they are

Her talent shines brighter than any star

Her drama skills are unmatched; she's a natural

Her improvisation is a delight to all

Her imagination runs wild like a mountain stream

Her every performance, a masterpiece, a dream

That amazing Julia, a girl of many gifts

Her talents are endless, her spirit uplifts

She shines like the sun, a light so bright

She's a living inspiration, a true delight

IT HAS TO BE

If love is thinking about someone all the time

Everywhere

Every way

Then I love…Jesus

But if love is a craving

That comes from deep within

Constantly increasing

Then I love…food

But if love is ups and downs

Caring, learning, experiencing

Then I love…life

But if love is wanting to share your life with someone

To care for and prayer for

If love is and it has to be

Or this world would make no sense at all

Then I love…you

NYC

If the prophets had seen New York

Their weeping would not have been for Jerusalem

Today, I saw so many things

All the people you could meet and never know

I heard the offers of the hookers,

the ladies of the street

Selling themselves like so much meat

And of course, the drunks

Who start something hurting inside me

Jesus said, "I was a drunk in a doorway

And you shook your head and never asked

Why must the world be this way?"

Then I saw your picture, J.C. in glorious three-D

Selling beside a dildo in some store window

Wicked city with no prophets left to stone

Why should God destroy you

When you seem to be doing that on your own.

L-O-V-E

L is for laughter and tears
    shared together throughout the years

O is being your only love and you mine
    which is so liberating

V is for vacant, for without you,
  life's metaphor is an empty hotel

E is for every day and every way I love you.
    Everything centers around you
        as I daily learn to set self-interest aside.

INSPIRED BY GINSBERG'S "HOWL"

I've watched the brightest minds of my generation
   melted by medical marijuana madness,
      fearful of the god's Global Warming end-game.
Destroyed by our own corporate greed,
 not unable but unwilling to make changes in time
 as the waters rise. Tears in our eyes blinded by the Starry
      Dynamo of broken dreams and colonies on Mars.
Where have all the angel-haired Hippies gone?
   Happy only to sing and dance and make love real.
 Paint your peace signs on the walls of the poor
 and realize you can't fight the missile makers,
 the arms dealers with their Doomsday Drones
 from The Military Industrial Complex.
Come sail the sea with us to see the flotsam-awesome
 plastic pieces that are our legacy.
We pollute the air, the land, the sea
 and stockpile enough Nuclear Weapons to make saving

the planet seem a senseless impossibility.

We have become numb, lost in the blue light of our video screens

   and dumb-ass smartphones,

 calling it connectivity while we suffer and live alone.

Give us this day our daily apps and games, click bait and

   Quantum Computers and we will overlook and forget the constant
   multiple murders and hate crime waking nightmares.

Promise us movie stars and crowded bars and crank up the music so
loud we can't think or contemplate our fearful fate in drug-induced
dreams.

We have no time to mourn the many who died when the earth shook
and the buildings collapsed to cover the corpses with tombstones of
concrete.

We busy ourselves conversing with Artificial Intelligent brains on
how to find love, hoping these machines are not secretly seeking to
destroy us.

Forgive us our poetry, our sins of indifference

and all the wasted time when we could have been learning

                              to care for each other,

   to solve some problems rather than ignore them,

To feed the hungry, house the homeless,

 protect the innocent creatures who strive only to survive

 the endless onslaught of inhumane humanity,

Friends, while you are not safe, I am not safe.

 You're not crazy if you can see how crazy this wicked and wacky world can be.

 If it concerns you as it does me.

If you sometimes feel lost in the madness,

 hurt by the cruelty, lonesome in the crowds.

If there is a God, you are in my prayers.

If you have a story to tell, I will listen.

ATTA BOY HONEST ABE

Am I not destroying my enemies

When I make friends with them?

I don't want my enemies dead

I was taught to love them instead

So Jesus did say

Though war seems reluctant to pass away

When peace is everything we need

Perhaps it's not about hate but more about greed

Business decisions and security

Mad over money and it's just me, me, me.

I'd rather follow Lincoln's line

And take all the world as friends of mine.

ODE TO FREEDOM

On the two-hundred and thirty-seventh birthday

 of my country, often called the Land of the Free,

I asked my friends what Freedom means to them.

One said it means nobody can tell you what to do.

Another said, it's the freedom to love who you want

and to make decisions for yourself.

It means being able to travel and live where you like.

Some mentioned the pursuit of happiness and human rights:

To live free from emotional or physical abuse.

One called freedom a cruel joke when America imprisons

more people than any other country in the world.

I think freedom means being able to gather with others

and having the right to express your thoughts on any topic

you choose. And perhaps most importantly, it's about

Freedom from Need, where everyone has enough food,

shelter and clean water.

Wc have come a long way and yet there is still far to go.

IT'S ONLY A QUESTION OF WHEN

If you're looking for signposts to heaven, consider this:

God made the world

And man made religions

God wrote his name across the stars

And man wrote the Koran and the Bible

And various Holy books

God tells us when we will be born

And when we will die

And man dares to tell us where we go then?

Leave it to God

It's just a question of when.

Let Alone My Heart

Been too long since I've written a poem

       with love inside it

I've considered myself unqualified

To write about love or even understand it

So, how I feel now will have to do

It's so hard to put your thoughts on paper

       Let alone your heart

But the thought of you won't leave my heart alone

Pardon me if my love is showing

Joy like this was meant to be overflowing

It feels so good to be so happy with you

       Without having to try

It just happens when we're together

       And I don't know why

But lately…even now

       My favorite word is "WOW!"

MY LIFE'S WINE

The glass of my life's wine

Teeters on the table edge of eternity

Until

Much against my will

It falls

Crimson drops spilling

Into a forever pool of light

Alright

You can't stop tears from the sky

I've had long enough to wonder why

I've known since I was young

We are born to die

Now, Whomever art in heaven

Please forgive me my sins

And let the journey begin.

Hunting

If I were a deer fleeting away at a run

Would you be a hunter behind a hunter's gun?

If I was a heart beating in fright

Would you be a bullet burning in flight?

If death found its mark and decided to stay

Would you pick up your gun

and be off on your way?

Visiterds

I give you fond aloha

Don't ask me for the moon

And now you must be going

Don't sing a heartbreak tune

I give you leis hand-woven

And send you off with nuts

Now, please get off my aching back

No ands, or ifs, or buts.

Audrey "Mom" Marantz

My Better Half

Sky so tall, ocean wide

I sit here with my love by my side

My companion through thick and thin

The better half of every mood I'm in

Night so dark, lights so bright

Darling, you make me feel alright

The music of your gentle touch,

The song I long to hear so much

Time so short, life so sweet

You're all the love I'll ever need

HAVEN'T WRITTEN A POEM

I haven't written a poem in a long time
It's not that there's not a thought in my head
Instead
I've busied myself
With gardens
And woodworking
Music

Even made a drum
From a huge hunk of a Royal Palm Tree
Far from ho-hum for me
Summer is not necessarily "free"

But it's a time for me to try new things
To spread my wings
And feel what fun it is to fly
Or at least try

CAN'T BEAT THE BEATLES

Coo Coo Ka Chew

Where's that Walrus?

Na na na nana na na, Hey Jude

Let it be, Be, Be, Be, Be the Beatles

Come together: shoot me through Diamond skies

Wonder whys

The music I knew as I grew

All came out Coo Coo Ka Chew

And if there is an eggman,

Then no one I think is in my tree, Obla-dee

Wanna be the Beatles

Grow me some long hair

All's fair in Love and Peace, Give it a chance

You may be a lover but can you dance?

What is the answer and should we sing?

That in the end, the love we take

is equal to the love we make.

Mambo Mamma

My, my, my, my Mambo Mamma
Choo choo choose me tonight
So, so, fa, fa, fine you are, evening star
Wanna make you fee, fee, feel alright
With mu, mu, music mixed with moonlight
Shh, shh, shh, shining serenely
My, my, my, melody finding flight
Now wow, wow is the time
My, my Mambo Mamma
Purr, purr perhaps we might
Da, da, dance or
Row, row, romance this night away
And purr, perhaps
Your lips on my mine
Will all, all, always stay.

STRICTLY PROSE

No Poetry

No, no sir-ee

Not a rhyming word or sound

Around here, my dear

Strictly prose

For those who know

No Poetry

And as for me

A man of means

A poem can say

More than it seems

So please compose

Much more than prose

For those who dream such dreams

HOW I WONDER

Scintillate,

Scintillate,

Subdiminutive

Fusion based

Hydrogen mass

How I speculate

As to your make-up

And function

Twinkle, twinkle

Little star

How I wonder

What you are

Out there in outer space

So far beyond the human race

FIFTY-EIGHT

Fifty-eight

Is great

So far

I'm a star in my car

Not crusin'

Usin' this time to rhyme

While I'm

Still young

My song sung

My life in song

Live long

Well past 58

And in the end,

The love you make

Is simply no mistake

JANUARY 1ST 2013

First day of the first month of lucky thirteen

If you know what I mean

Don't need luck: got me a piece of destiny

Someone's looking out for me

Love is on a roll: time will take its toll

But in my head, I'm free

Knowing what's right helps us through it

The only thing is to do it

Knowing love wins is assuring

Though the ways of the world are alluring

All you need is love

Learned that from the Beatles (and Above)

I'm looking forward to all I can do

My way or the highway of Thy way?

Time will tell

Hopin' for heaven

Fit for hell

Done with teachin'

Might try preachin'

Just as well

Silent, thoughtful compassion

Charity, peace, hope, consideration

A new nation conceived in liberty

A perfect fit for me

Even if I'm only imagining I'm free

'Tis enough just to be

My best buddy's Mom

Gave me a wonderful compliment when she told me

"You were always a loving child."

That's wild, that's cool, I'm a fool for love

What better goal can one man need

To know there's love in me

And I want it to grow

Yes, I want to know all the love I can be

And like the Bible says,

Love sets us free

MISTAKES

Mistakes?

    I've made a few

Those are the sort of things the curious are bound to do

    And it can be a learning experience if you're aware

      It can help you through

        I should know by now. I've had more than a few

Love that never could be

    There's a limit to just how free

      One can act

        There are facts

          Opinions

            Ideas

              It's true

But I have to answer to no one but God

    And you, my wife

    And that makes for a good life

CHRISTMAS JUST PAST

The ghost of Christmas past

Is but a few moments before

And before I forget

I wrote this to remember…

Emily bursting forth

From a big box

Much to Juju's delight

Followed by tickle time

With young faces all aglow

Smiles, surprises and fun

Family and friends

All as it should be

And me, sleeping away

Before the party ends

Guess I'm getting old, friends

CREATIVELY CRAZY

Reduced to this belly-button lint sculpture

Creatively crazy, lazy artist, art this, Art Thou, Art now

Politically correct

The words direct the flow

And sometimes even I don't seem to know

Where it all leads. (all creatures bleed)

All you need is love; love is yes indeed

Prolonged rhyme stuck in time

Rhythm in him and his hymn of praise

I raise my poet's hands in awe of the greatest

Creator of all, Heavenly poem,

Give us this day our daily day we pray and let us play

There's time enough for something to say

Thanks comes to mind and what can I do for You?

So ends this poet's poem or prayer

With a Holy Hallelujah and a "Hope You're there."

2018

Frogs croak

  The jokes on us

The nights for song

  Can we sing along?

All night long

  Tick and Tock

    This amphibian clock

      Chimes the time and rhymes

        As geckos click in

And it's more where you are

Than where you've been

<u>BENCH WARMER</u>

Don't be a bench-warmer for Jesus

 Gotta get in the game

If you call yourself a Christian

 Gotta live up to His Name

If you gotta Good Book

 But it stays on the shelf

  For months on end…

   My friend,

    You should be

     Ashamed of yourself.

A Prayerful Poem

This is a prayerful poem
    To wish you strength
        Food, a job, a home
            To see the joy
                To not be alone

To find your skills
    To be a part
        To share your beliefs
            And share your heart

Finally free
    With lots to do
        Time to pray
            And just me and you

LITERARY EDIFICATION?

Oh Poet, please

What have you done?

Forsaken Literary Edification

Content to have fun

Laughter to soothe the mind

Lots to say

Plenty of time

To think

To write

To share

Right here

Yet getting somewhere

Freedom awaits on this blank page

The freedom to speak,

That's Democracy's stage

Heaven and Hell

To dwell with saints above
Oh, that will be glory

To dwell below
With those we know
Well, that's a different story

Heaven is eternal
Or so the Bible does say

But give me just a moment in Hell
And I could learn to pray

Heaven or Hell, the choice is yours
But I'm hoping to land on those Heavenly shores

LONG LASTING LOVE

In the quiet of morning

    Before the dawn breaks

        My thoughts wander about

            About you

                About us

                    And our long-lasting love

You complete me

    Improve me

        Protect me from myself

You let me be

    And let me be myself

        As I support you

            What a team

What a marvelous dream we are together

    And may we be together as long as life lasts

Join Me In Some Words

Wherever we are

    Mountain, sea, home

        It takes but a spark

            To ignite a poem

If you have the inclination

    Imagination

    Time

Join me in some words

    That rhyme

    And together

        We poets will be

    Me and you

You and me

<u>RAIN</u>

Rain is a blessing

    The Lord's way of saying I love you

        (or I could drown you)

I prefer a gentle mist that lands on my lashes

    I can look up and feel it caressing my eyes

Sometimes it paints a rainbow or two

    With the golden light of dawn

Against a backdrop of cliffs, our comfortable cove/home

Then there's heavy rain,

    The kind a tropical rain forest is famous for

        It keeps flowing; everything green keeps growing

            While the waterfalls sing white noise of peace

And just when you think it couldn't rain harder,

    It starts pouring down to beat the band

        And that's God saying He really loves you (a lot)

Bathe the Earth clean with your showers

Sky and cloud, thunder loud

The wet dreams of flowing streams to thirsty seas

Please don't let us be washed away

Flooded, ark-less

To sink or swim

But it's just rain

I will survive

I'm still alive… so far

My final retort:

Weather Report

Oh yes, it's still raining.

FIND A WAY

I only want to say

We should find a way

To love our Lord with all we've got

With all He is and all we're not

And love each other as we should

To do our best to do some good

What a world it will be

When everyone's free

Compassion and caring

And everyone's sharing

When God runs the show

Let everyone know

The day's coming fast

When we will all love at last

Sweet Lord Almighty, love at last

TOO EARLY?

Is it ever too early to write a poem?

Sitting at home as I often do

I could say it's a poem for you

But it isn't and it isn't for me

It's for my country, my 'tis of thee

Our hope for liberty, our goal of unity

Our chance for a more loving destiny

When we no longer focus on what's wrong

But keep in sight what's good and right

Treat others as we might like to be treated

A country not defeated by strife

But dedicated to a good life for all

For all Americans, I know we can

But we decide, a house divided cannot stand

Kindness for our fellow man

A place to be, free to believe as we choose

This is too precious to lose.

TRANSHUMANISM

God said I'm gonna make me a man

And Adam began, made of mud

And is, to this day, still dumb as dirt

You can see it in our willingness to hurt

In war after war, like so many before

I'm not sure if this "Civilized Society" will ever find peace

But it seems like we can if we get our heads out of the sand

Can we trust humans to create a better man?

There's still so much we don't understand

You don't need to splice my genes

To teach me it's not good to be mean

I don't need no nano-machines inside

To understand the dangers of prejudice and pride

Who determines the kind of 'improvement' we need?

Will we be motivated by compassion or corrupted by greed?

It might be alright to experiment to prevent disease

But don't go making any super-humans, please

Unstuck

So many poems

So little time

Rarely alone

Hung up on rhyme

Billy Pilgrim poet has come unstuck in time

So many dreams

So little me

Rarely a poet

So often free

To think or tinker with words and sound

Roderoo the poet has been reborn and unbound

Three cheers for Vonnegut

Cat's Cradle's so cool

It inspired me to write some books

Am I an author or a fool?

FOR UNCLE IRA

A good man is loving

Is a person of his word

Is kind and giving to others

Is Joyful

Thankful

Humble

Forgiving

And Forgiven

Thoughtful

Purposeful and Persistent

Dependable and Honest

Reverent

Contemplative and Questioning

A good man produces good fruit

Remains balanced, centered

Always looking for the right thing to do or say

He doesn't waste a day, doesn't forget to pray

Still remembers how to play

Refrain From the Mundane

Allow me to play with my brain
  Refrain from the mundane reality of thinking
    there is only one way the world has to be
Make imagination a meaningful part of me
  Set my imprisoned soul free
What amazing things I might do
  I could conceive of something new
See this life in a different way
  Discover new things I so need to say.
Appreciate the amazement of all the awe surrounding me
  Not only what is but what this can be
    When we look with new eyes and learn how to see
When life brings us to tears for the beauty beholden
  And love overflows; yes these moments are golden
This is the power of what possibly can be
  This future of hope that awaits you and me
    When we open our minds, take the time to conceive it
We can change our whole world when we finally believe it.

JOY

Joy lives on playgrounds

Between stars and castle clouds

At sunrise in loving eyes

Joy says, "Seven days with no laughter makes one weak."

It's light as a morning mist on your face

Thrilling as riding a wave to shore

It's whistles and giggles

Bird songs and love songs and screams of delight

A breeze through the trees at night

Joy is a child smiling from ear to ear

Blowing dandelion blossom wishes on the wind

Joy wears moonbeam scarves and rainbow suspenders

Flowers in its hair and sea shells on its shoes

It tastes like frosty iced tea on a sizzling summer's day

Perfect with popcorn and pizza

You just want to say, "Come joy. Stay. Let's play"

LIFE'S BEEN GOOD TO ME

A small town childhood, climbing apple trees

> Cooling off in a creek

> > Church sing-alongs

A sweet sixteen Salvation Sunday

> Falling so hard in love

> > Acting in plays, so many roles throughout my days

College and Amsterdam, Rugby and gymnastics

> Learning and loving

> > Social work and drama workshops

> > Cross country adventures

Commercial fishing in my Hawaiian home

> Songwriting and recording

> > Finding my family

> > Making movies

> > > Improv comedy and sorrow

Shaping a rainforest and kayaking coastlines

> Writing plays and books

> > Hard to believe where I've been and all I've done

> > It's sure been fun

STILL GOIN'

I'm what happens when two loving parents

Let their kid have lots of experiences and travel

Church time and gifts and advice

But let him make up his own mind

I'm a product of who I've met, what I learned

Mistakes I've made, values I've chosen

Where I've lived and who I've loved

How I spend my time and what genes I've got

What germs I've beaten and things I won't do

All I've eaten, sports I've tried, even the times I've lied

Every song I wrote, my time on boats

Bikes and toys and joys and occasional tears

Sixty-some years and still goin'

Still growin'

Not done learnin' and yearnin'

Dreamin' and schemin'

And how I love to play

Yes, I'm glad for each day

HOW I THINK, I THINK

There are and will always be

    Greater minds than mine

        And I don't mind that

It does not prevent me from wondering

    What goes on inside my head

My head may say, "Follow your heart."

    But my heart is silent in most matters except love

It's my mind that must make sense of all I see

    Hear, touch, smell and taste (always smell before tasting)

    It's in my head that all logic, creativity and curiosity lies

All laughter starts here, and grand schemes and future dreams

My mind seems to often converse with itself

    I often wonder this: if I consider all the times I think

        Of things that haven't happened (say, peace on Earth)

    Then I am creating a playground for my mental gymnastics

Each of us builds our own distinctly different world

With all we've learned, mistakes endured

From the sane to the absurd

By reading and talking and sometimes… listening

I often speak without thinking (no filter)

I think when I'm alone

Even when meditatively trying not to think at all

And though I may not be the sharpest shovel in the shed,

I, like everyone else, can think as I please

It is upon such freedoms as these

We dictate or create imperfect democracies

I think thinking is fun

I am but one

But not the only one

Others may disagree

But they hold no sway over me

SAND IN YOUR MOUTH

Sorrow lies

   In darkness

      Whispering

         "I can have you

            Ruin you

       You don't dare mess with me.

   I'll be all your fears

      Flooded by tears

   A voice of negativity

      Scraping my fingernails

         Across the blackboard of your hopes

Dressed in cold sweat and chains

   I'll be the sand in your mouth

      Tormented thoughts of going nowhere."

But I say to you Sorrow, "You are not me

   And someday Sorrow, I will be free!"

HECK-NO-LOGIC, TECHNO-LOGIC

Buy it, Use it, Break it, Fix it,

Lose it, Drop it, View it, Screw it,

Print it, Dent it, Drag and drop it, How you stop it?

Scrunch it, Scoot it, Best reboot it

Arrange it, Change it, Work it harder

Rename it, Game it, Make it longer

If you can't face it, best erase it. Technology Apology

It's the least they can do to you and me.

We've come too far. This is who we are

Tell me what you got? Tell me what I'm not

How'd you get so hot? I put you on the spot

Are you game or what? Look at the time,

your place or mine?

Gotta get it up, somethin' to prove, gotta get with it,

get in the groove. Gotta get it on, come on and move,

Tech-no-logic, heck-no-logic

V-Ball

Bump, Set, Slam, Dig

        Wahine Volleyball is very big.

        Just ask the crowds who wait in line.

Just ask that darling girl of mine.

      Serve, Pass, Set, Kill

Will they win?

         You know they will.

Dink, Dive, Shout, Scream!

    We support our Rainbow Team.

Jump, Block, Roof, Cheers!

    This could surely be our year.

Watch The Wave,

Around it goes,

Our way of saying

Let's go Bows!

Braggin'

I'm a good poet

    Well, not just good…

        And 'great' doesn't quite cover it

'Outstanding' comes close

    As does 'magnificent'

        Though I prefer 'unparalleled'.

(Most any superlative is always appreciated)

Though I don't need others singing my poetic praises

    To maintain my sense of competent accomplishment

        Frankly, words themselves fail to adequately describe

            the poetic pinnacles of satiric success I have achieved,

                or so I believe

        Which is in itself ironic and a paradox

Since words themselves are the very tools I employ

    to express my thoughts,

        My emotions and memories,

        To describe life's mysteries,

To analyze,

And categorize,

And dramatize

Each occurrence and endeavor that catches my fancy.

And though, it's true, I don't need the praise…

Yet, I humbly accept it

As a necessary result

Of unintended greatness on my part

When you honor me, you honor my art

AMERICA'S DIVERSITY

We the People,

Citizens of all backgrounds and creeds,

Uniquely different, yet Americans all the same.

Our love for our Country remains.

Long live liberty! Yes, liberty through diversity.

Us Athletes and Welfare Mothers,

Old Folks and Astronauts,

Farmers and Free Thinkers,

Cub Scouts and Drop Outs,

Prisoners and Pioneers.

We each make up America the Beautiful,

And each, in his and her own way,

Define and defend Freedom for All.

And it takes all kinds,

All kinds of people,

Each unlike any other,

Unique so to speak.

Expectant Mothers and Black Power Brothers,

Entertainers and Explainers, Teachers and Preachers.

Together, we determine what it means to be,

the Land of the Free.

This Nation of Immigrants and Refugees,

who have found a home, a safe place to be.

The Veterans and Pacifists,

Scientists and Pessimists,

Rednecks and Hipsters,

Indians and Engineers,

Toddlers and Smooth Talkers.

The Homeless and the Wealthy,

The Sick and the Healthy,

Introverts and Extroverts.

For all our quirks and imperfections,

We're united in our shared affection,

For this Country that we call Home,

From sea to sea, with room to roam.

Us Writers and Fighters and Hikers and Bikers,

Police with big sticks,

Poets with word tricks.

      Let's hear it for Converts and Convicts!

The Deaf, the Dumb, the Blind: all kinds!

Politicians! Morticians! Mormons on missions!

      Street Musicians to please us,

            Lawyers to squeeze us.

      It astounds the imagination

how many different minds and kinds of people

      it takes to make a Nation, this Nation.

So let's give thanks to the Men and Women

      who lay down their lives in war after war,

        no matter what those wars are for.

Give thanks to all those Nine-to-fivers,

      The Late Arrivers,

        The Holocaust Survivors,

      Who keep plugging away.

Who are willing to pay

      For our multiple sins,

        or our marvelous deeds.

God bless every Soul Searching Soul in need.

Every Man, Woman, Boy and Girl,
Who make this such an Interesting World.

NICE ADVICE

Show kindness

Stay humble

Express gratitude

Be courageous

Stay curious

Appreciate nature

Love unconditionally

Celebrate life

Be honest

Embrace change

Keep learning

Nurture relationships

Encourage others

Be patient

Laugh often

Find Peace

Happy B-Day JC

Happy birthday, Jesus Christ

Peace on Earth would sure be nice

And lots of love to see us through

And meaningful things for us to do

Family, more friends, adventures galore

To learn things we didn't know before

Quiet times and times to sing

Each wonderful moment that Christmas brings

One day at a time, that's not too much

Kind words and a gentle touch

Eyes to see the beauty around us

Music and art and all that astounds us

Bless all the mothers and fathers, sisters and brothers

You were right to say we should love one another

Even the lost, the lonely, downtrodden and forlorn

Thanks, Baby Jesus, I'm so glad you were born

FOR JANIE

You deserve a Christmas poem
You, who make our house a home
You cook and clean and shop and plan
And do your best to love your man

For life's big decisions, we turn to you
And even the smaller decisions too
Such a hard worker, an example to all
All packed into a package so small

Our wonderful Nana, such love and care
Our lives are better because you're there
You're the finest gift we could ever wish for
Because you keep on giving,
who could ask for more?

GOD HAS A PLAN

God has a plan for each of us; for me

But how to find the key to unlock this game

Of holy hide and seek?

Must I be merciful?

Or meek?

Must I pray or fast?

How long will the assignment last?

Am I up to the task?

Is it all tied up with a heavenly reward?

What if I get bored?

Will the directions be clear?

Can I get there from here?

Can I pick and choose?

If I snooze do I lose?

What if I fail?

Can't He just send me an E-mail?

Or give me a call?

That's all.

THE NEED FOR EXCESS

There's enough.

Enough space,

Enough food,

Enough money,

Enough good things to do,

to create.

But not enough to satisfy some people's greed:

their need for excess, the trappings of fame.

How many know my name?

Am I winning the game?

And if I win, must others lose?

Is this the life we'll choose?

Where can we find an educated, compassionate,

moral society?

Ask someone drunk with greed and they may say:

"Fuck sobriety."

THE MOST AMAZING DREAM

Dear Heart, last night I had the most amazing dream
   In what I'll call my Imagination Museum

Obviously, we create our dreams
   Though not in any predetermined way
      I consider dreams to be the mind at play

Anyway, there I was in what felt like a museum-type setting
   Marble columns and subdued lighting
Imagining mind over matter manipulation of my surroundings
   Inanimate stone brought to life
      Slow motion fluid movement through distorted time
The music of stars, the power of awe, a oneness of joy and being
Seeing so clearly what cannot be remembered in passing of time
I'm simply left with a hint of the Creator's power to amuse
How quickly confusing it all seems in the light of day
   Still, I'm willing to say,
      Perhaps I transcended dimensions

But as I mentioned at the start, I was only dreaming, dear heart.

If I could change the world

Last night, I had the strangest dream

I imagined my imagination had the power to shape reality, OK?

And it seems true that we must imagine first,

Think things through before we act

Consciously conceive an idea before we can take steps

To make things happen

Whether to create or just change our outlook

or modify our thinking

And while dreaming I got to thinking

how I would change the world

if only imagining could make it so, so…

I thought it would be fun to change all nuclear armaments

Into chocolate so children could eat them up

and enjoy a sugar rush while saving the world

Guns would never again shoot bullets, only butterflies.

Humankind would blend bodies and colors,
nationalities and ideals
into a unity of mutual support
building a paradise

And you too can dream.
Isn't that nice?

GODS/gods

"You shall have no other gods before me…."
But if there's only one God, how can that be?
Is it God-like to display jealousy?

Father God, what happened to mother?
One God lonesome with no other.

In your image, made you us
Do you also kill and cuss?

Envy, lust and gluttony
Are you just the same as me?

Lord almighty, you made the place
I hope you're happy with the human race

As It Was…

Man versus Nature

Honestly…I hope the Earth wins

I'm bettin' on it; just ask the dinosaurs what our odds are

Old Mother Earth's been 'round and round

     for a long, long time

Molten and sea-soaked, forested and frosted

Nestled in her sweet spot,

    in just enough sunshine for life to spring

      For birds to sing, for fish to swim

        Every her and him

          Yes, humans too

            This earthy zoo

Such violent ones

    But aren't they fun?

      With their gods and art

        Agriculture and industry

          The only ones to write down history

To believe in immortality

    Knowing the sun will grow to consume all eventually

      Earth with Nature, no mother she'll be

    Just rock and iron spinning as it was in the beginning

Spinning through a dark and endless

        star-filled sea of nothingness

HEAVEN AWAITS

Gonna die

Wanna live

Everyone dies

Not everyone lives

Don't mind dying

Sure like living

Want to see the other side

Want to live fully

Wanna die peacefully

Wanna live peacefully

Not too scared of dying

Sometimes scared of livin'

Heaven awaits

But I can wait.

ANY QUESTIONS?

Let's give kids wings. Don't give me stats.

    No data do dis or data does dats

Let's ask ourselves how we can prepare the kids

        for a nuclear-free future?

          Teach them to love.

Why is there no talk of ecological lessons

    as we swelter in our global warming classrooms?

       Where do we stand on the fate of man?

Do we teach the pursuit of happiness or what freedom can mean?

    Do we freely speak our minds or toe the line?

Are we narrowing our focus in an ever-expanding world?

    Do we teach to tests imposed by a failed presidency?

Must they only read and compute or can they create and dream?

    Do we ponder the complexity of the universe

       or play politics with their young minds?

Do we celebrate the diversity of cultures

    or sing my country right or wrong?

Have we shown the children the peace of meditation,

the sense of oneness of being out in nature?

Is History to be found in a list of battles

or in a compilation of our art and accomplishments?

Have we taught them to learn, to get by without us?

Can they balance their budgets better than the government?

Dare we lead them to clear, logical, tolerant, global thinking?

Do we box them in or show them how to think outside the box?

Are they thinking about our future? Thinking for the fun of it?

Thinking so they won't be fooled or manipulated?

Do we want to see them become free thinkers or cannon fodder?

Do we teach them to deal with stress, alienation, and depression?

Have they learned to listen to each other, to think before speaking?

Do they respect others, question authority, laugh, sing and play?

Are we stealing their childhood away? Who has the final say?

Is learning relevant?

Is a 'good job' to be their only goal?

Have we taught them compassion or crushed their spirits?

Have we forgotten to laugh and forgive?

Are we preparing them or boring them?

Are we molding them into a submissive citizenry?

Do we just want them to sit down and be quiet?

What shall we tell them of terror, lust and greed?

Shall we warn them of the military-industrial complex

or the folly of war?

Are they too young or are we too late?

Can they recognize our biases, our bullshit?

Are they here to exercise their brains

or develop their imaginations?

Do we want them just to be reading response robots

and mathematical monsters?

Who will care for us in times to come, heal our hurts,

sculpt our gardens, write our novels, protect our wilderness,

care for the oceans, find new solutions?

Now that we can communicate faster and farther,

have we found anything meaningful to say?

Are we asking the right questions?

Pointing them in the right direction?

What is our plan?

Who gets to decide?

What do you think?

DAD'S ADVICE

The Mrs. has got me on a short leash

Spending little

Less and less

Oh, yes

(unless she wants to)

What can one do?

Born to serve

More blessings than I deserve

Sixty years young

Watching my father fade

Ninety-two and it could happen to you

Or so I'm told

And Dad looked me in the eye

And said,

"Don't get old."

That was his advice for me

And then he checked out at ninety-three.

Quite a Thrill

Fight and kill

Oh, yes we will

It's quite a thrill

And still

Someday… war will end

And we'll be left with nothing…

but friends.

"Seven Ways to Look at an Eagle"

A living, flying symbol of my nation home

This magnificent, majestic creature of a benevolent Creator

Pine-perched watcher of the morning light

A predatory raptor soaring over the sea

White head and tail built to sail the sky

A high-pitched communicating commander of an island forest

Streaking between towering pines.

All the fun of flight

Both Within and Without

Just to say, "Life is great!"

Fails to capture

The sentiment

Completely

It begs for examples

Morning sun and bird song

Freedom to be and do

A family's love

And a certain peace

Both within and without

An attitude of gratitude

A Saturday in June

2016

SHE'S THE LOVE

She may not be

As stunning to you

As she is to me

I see past the years

I am used to her tears

Her tone

Her voice

I benefit from the haircuts

And back scratches

Meals and movies

Corrections and imperfections

She's the love in my songs

The light in each morning

I've never known better

And need no one more

I know her now and what our love is for

"AnyWho Lived"

(Inspired by e.e.cummings' "Anyone Lived in a Pretty How Town")

AnyWho lived

in a quiet country jungle

(occasional bird song floating, countless chirps up)

Sun, rain, wind, stillness

Friends and family

(both here and near)

Affectionately frolic and dine

Tell their stories, give of their time

Clouds, sun, moon, stars

Children grow

(upward and inward, this side and that)

Dawn, day, sunset, dark

Love to spare

My wonderful wife, my mate

Comforting, heart felt fine

Tears by joy, moments by years

Surely meant to be mine

There will be loves fallen into,

Working and complaining,

Singing and laughing,

Dozing, daydreaming, dismal, dazzling

Wearing their smiles with abandon

Hot, cold, night, bright

and only the mountains remember

floating cloud sun-showers

Stand up tall

One day comes my time

(some may notice)

I'll be ashes across sea and hill

I know I will

Heaven by hope, something in everything

Now and then and if by chance

You think of me

Sing a song and dance a dance

And I will always be

Us and Them, (Yea and Yo!)

Autumn, Summer, Winter, Spring

(blissfully blessed, little pain)

Moon, stars, sun, rain

A DAY FOR DANA

Aloha and Hawaiian chanted

We gather as family and friends to remember Dana

To share in her passing to the next adventure

Adding our prayers to the reverend's

Prayers that are ours
While Dana is now the stars
The light
The day and night
A bit of it all
No matter how immense
Or how small

Scripture: know He loves us
Nothing can defeat this because love wins

JC said, "Don't let your hearts be troubled.

I go to prepare a place for you…"
So we can be together
Dana's Dudly shares memories of her sister
She senses her presence still
She recalls growing up and together
Kid's crazy times
Walks in nature
Life challenges and caring for their mother, Lynne

Dana's daughter, Alexis
Speaks softly
Unsure of what form her mom now takes on
She shares a poem of ends and beginnings

Love is winning

Dana's husband, Gary
Tells how she put others first
How she never knew a stranger
How she exemplified caring
Forgiveness of sins
Love always wins

Dana was kind

And giving

Though no longer living,

Her next step is taken

What's next begins

Love wins

MY SALVATION SITUATION

Are you saved?

Saved.

Five letters

Add an "L" and it becomes 'slaved'

As in enslaved

Some I've seen seem enslaved by their faith

It occupies them completely

Compelled to tell others…

It's not that way with me

I may be saved:

Prayed the prayer

and have prayed since

but I don't brag about it

or completely understand it.

Besides, humility better suits humanity.

So if you want to talk to me of spiritual matters,

You may have to be the one to start that conversation.

Salvation?

Saved from what?

From evil?

From unkind words or deeds?

Saved means I'm forgiven my wrongs

my mistakes,

the harm I've done,

chances for good I've missed.

Saved,

Forgiven,

Offered eternity

Free.

That's what being saved means to me.

Nothing Better

There's nothing better for the human soul
For patience and humility

For learning to love and care
And be there in the moment

Nothing

No thing better

Than petting a cat. Imagine that.

CONFINED TO A VOID

Met my maker on Meth Mountain

And Satan said:

I'll grow crystals on your lungs

Trading your teeth for sleepless nights

Pornographic delights

Thin as a rail

Night-light pale

Confined to a void

Paranoid

Worship at my feet

No need eat

Meth breath that kills

Better than pills

When it all ends with you dead,

Remember what I said

Speed kills

I PUT THE DUMB IN WISDOM

The real me

The one you may never see

Is legion

No demons

But quite a variety

The actor,

Musician,

Poet and playwright,

One of those unconditional love kind of Christians

An old man with his wilted words of wisdom

I put the 'dumb' in 'wisdom'.

MOSQUITO PHOTO

Bite me

Suck my blood

It's your nature

And you are nature

As am I

So fly mosquito

Don't alight

Or I might whack you

Attack you back

All's fair in this here war

And frankly

I can't stand anymore

Of your buzzin', cousin

POEM WAITING

There's a poem waiting
>In your willing heart

Hidden between the words
>So as not to offend

Immersed in metaphor mayhem
>To bring out a smile

Wrapped up in the love of syntax and syllables
>The magic of language

Smothered in love like simile pancakes in thick maple syrup
>For you, always for you

There's a love poem in here somewhere

THREE SQUARES AND A BED

I'm happy here

But that's just me

I'm determined to be

I know there are all kinds of hunger

And though I can't feed my head

I've got three squares and a bed

I remain mind-over-matter-free

Because

Because I am

Because I am determined to be

And that's just me